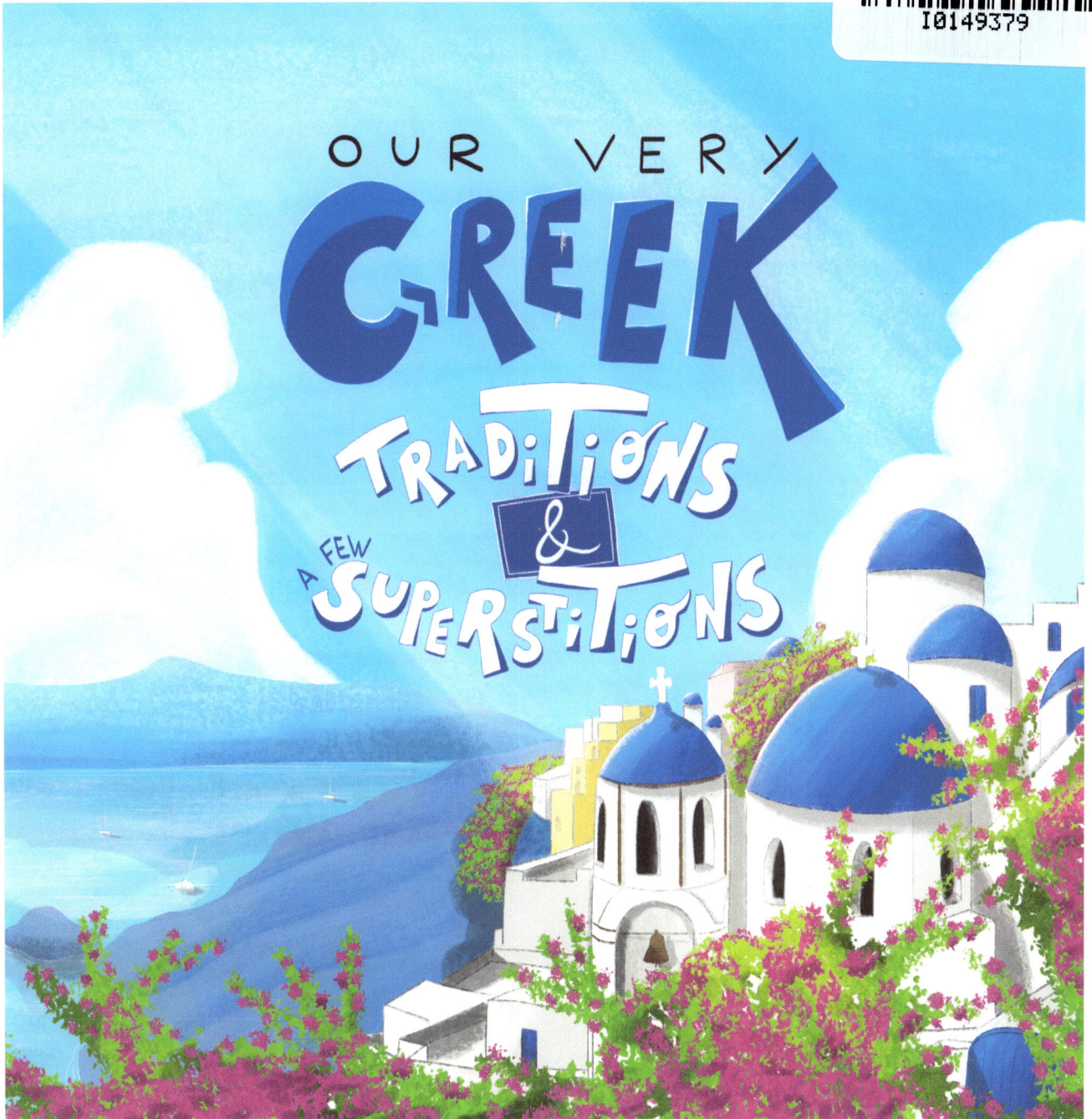

OUR VERY

GREEK

TRADITIONS
&
A FEW
SUPERSTITIONS

Published by
Adventuresome Words
Northumberland
England
www.adventuresomewords.com
info@adventuresomewords.com

First published by Adventuresome Words in 2025.
Text and illustrations copyright © Kassi Psifogeorgou. 2025.
Illustrator: Laura Mocelin.

Kassi Psifogeorgou
Our very Greek Traditions and a Few Superstitions
ISBN: 978-1-7384405-8-0

Purple Dragonfly Book Award
SM
WINNER

Dedication

To all the little ones who love our Greek stories.
May these tales fill your hearts with happiness and
help you feel proud of our traditions.

Have you ever heard of a name day?

In our sunny land by the deep blue sea, many people are named after saints, and each saint has a special day in the calendar. That day is called their "name day"—and if you share the saint's name, it's your celebration too!

On your name day, friends, neighbors, and family come to visit, bringing you gifts, and there's always plenty of delicious food and treats for everyone. Sounds exciting, doesn't it?

KEFTEDES

DOLMADES

New school year

LEAF BRANCHES

HOLY WATER

The school year starts with Ayiasmos. It's a special ceremony. A priest comes to the school and blesses the students and teachers with holy water. He dips the leaves in the holy water and sprinkles it over everyone.

We all gather in the courtyard, feeling excited, waiting to get our new books and meet new friends.

'Ohi' Day

In October, we celebrate Ohi Day on the 28th. It's a special day when we remember how Greece said "No" to the Italian invaders during World War II, refusing to let them take control of our land.

We wave flags, march in parades, and feel proud of our country's bravery.

The Mischievous Christmas Kalikatzari

In December, stories "come to life" with the arrival of the Kalikantzari. They live underground all year, but at Christmas, they come up to dance, play, and cause mischief while staying hidden...

KALI KATIZARI

MELOMAKARONA

KOURABIEDES

.. Until Theophania, when the priest blesses the water, making it holy and clean, and sends the Kalikantzari back to where they came from for the rest of the year.

***

Theophania is an important day in Greece because it celebrates the time when Jesus was baptized.

People also dive into the water to catch the cross, which is a special symbol of Christ's baptism.

It's believed that whoever catches the cross will be blessed with good health and luck for the year ahead.

But wait! Let's take a step back and see what happens in the first hours of New Year's Day.

We cut the Vasilopita, a special cake for Agios Vasilis. Inside, we hide a coin, and whoever finds the piece with the coin will have good luck all year!

We also smash a pomegranate at the door, and its seeds scatter everywhere. The more seeds, the more luck we get for the new year.

And finally, the luckiest person is the one who enters the house first in the new year. Remember to lead with your right foot!

VASILOPITA

New Year's Day

Apokries

When Carnival season comes, the streets are full of joy! In Patras, there are big parades with colorful floats and music. Both kids and adults paint their faces and dress up in beautiful costumes.

But in many parts of Greece, the celebrations are different because each area has its own unique way of celebrating.

GALAXIDI CARNIVAL

CARNIVAL IN ZAKYNTHOS

Clean
Monday

On Clean Monday, the sky fills with colorful kites flying high and spinning in the wind.

Families gather for picnics, playing in fields and meadows, enjoying a fun day together.

It marks the start of Lent, the 40-day fasting period before Orthodox Easter Sunday.

Instead of eating meat, people enjoy these traditional foods:

- Lagana: A special flatbread baked only on Clean Monday.
- Taramosalata: A creamy dip made from fish roe.
- Dolmades: Grape leaves filled with rice and herbs.
- Fasolada: A bean soup.
- Halvas: A sweet dessert made from semolina.

Martaki

When March starts, we make little red and white bracelets called 'Martis' or 'Martaki' to bring good luck and welcome spring.

Older people say they also help us not get sunburned from the bright sun.

The name 'Martis' comes from 'Martios,' which is the Greek word for March.

25th of March

 March 25th is an important day for both the country and the church.

 A long time ago, Greece was controlled by the Ottoman Empire. The Greek people didn't want to be controlled anymore, so they bravely fought to be free. After many years, they won their freedom and became a free country again.

 On this day, we have parades, wave flags, and tell stories about bravery and hope.

 We also celebrate when Angel Gabriel told Mary that she would have a baby, Jesus.

GREEK INDE

Easter

Easter in Greece is full of beautiful traditions.
You can find red eggs and sweet tsoureki everywhere.

On Holy Saturday, when the clock strikes midnight, everyone shouts
"Christos Anesti!" and the candles light up the night.

Easter in Greece is truly magical!

1st of May

And here we are, it's May Day, another special day. Families go out to the green fields to pick wildflowers, like daisies and poppies.

They make wreaths and hang them on their doors for good luck. This shows that spring has come to stay, bringing happiness to everyone. People also have a barbecue to share with family and friends.

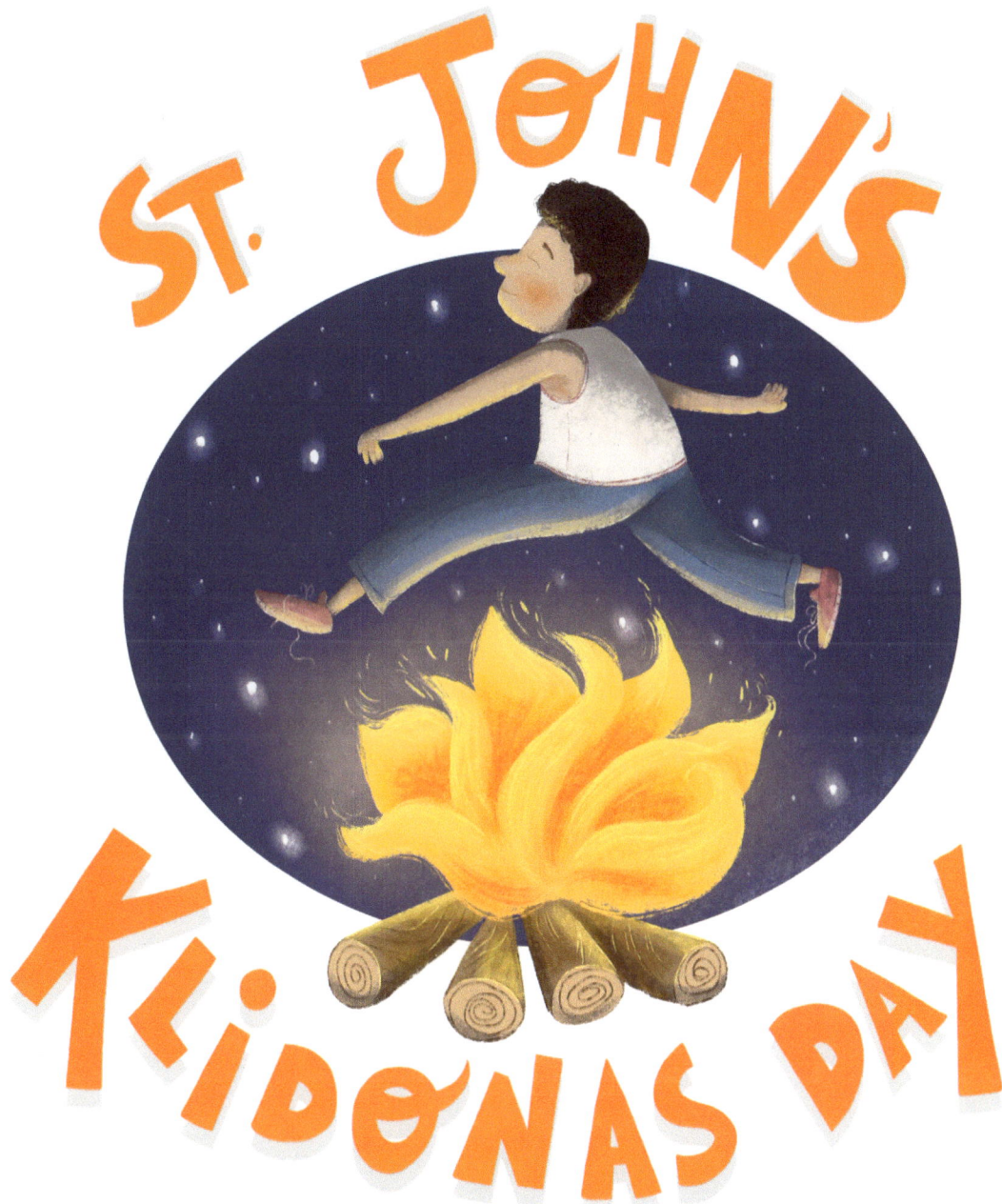

ST. JOHN'S

KLIDONAS DAY

In some areas, the wreaths stay up until June 24th for the St. John's Klidonas celebration. On that night, people burn the wreaths and jump over the flames three times for good luck and health.

15th of August

On August 15th, we remember Panagia (the Virgin Mary) and her journey to heaven. It's a day when people come together to honor her.

Some choose to fast before the celebration, but afterward, many enjoy traditional foods like lamb, roasted goat and souvlaki.

In village squares, there is dancing, eating, and celebrating, just like Easter Sunday, but on a smaller scale.
We call it 'Little Easter.'

Time for a few SUPERSTITIONS

Mati (means eye)

Have you heard about the Mati? When someone admires you or feels a bit jealous, they might give you the Mati, which can make you feel a little strange, like getting a headache.

But we have a secret to keep the Mati's tricks away! A deep blue charm with a bright eye helps protect us.

You can wear it around your neck, on your wrist, or hang it by your door. It's a playful guardian that keeps you safe from the Mati!

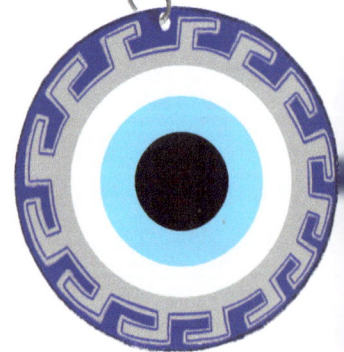

And if you think that's all, just wait! In Greece, spitting is believed to help keep bad luck away.

When someone gives you a compliment but might not mean it, or if they say something bad may happen, we say "ftou, ftou, ftou!" to keep a headache or bad luck from coming your way.

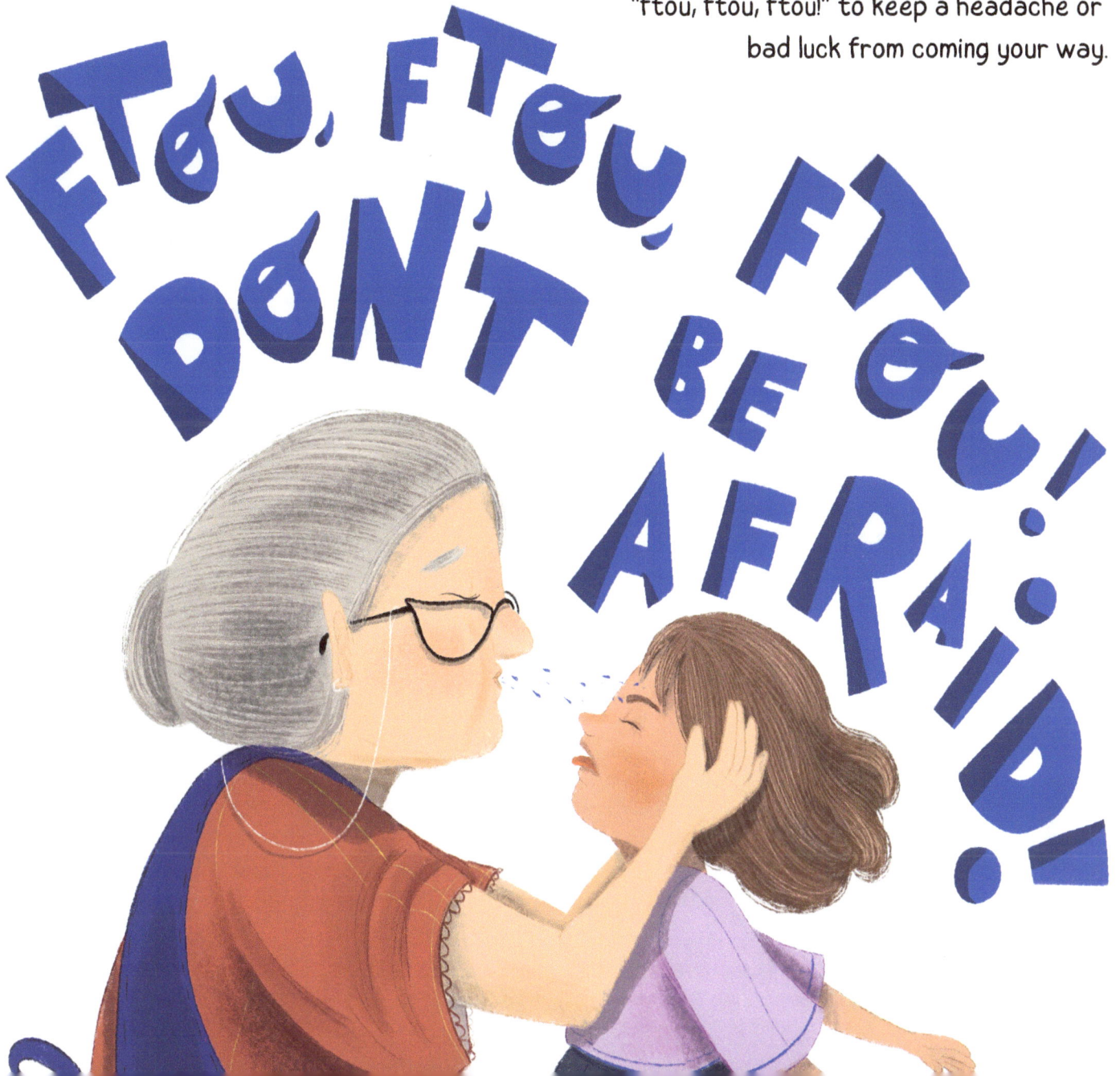

FTOU, FTOU, FTOU! DON'T BE AFRAID!

Black cat

Oh, and watch out! If you see a black cat, people say it brings bad luck for the rest of your day.

So, if you spot a black kitty on your path, you might want to take a different route to stay safe!

If you say the same thing as someone else at the same time, quickly shout "Piase kokkino!" and touch something red as fast as you can.

This helps to stop any arguments before they start and keeps things happy!

LET'S LEARN SOME
FACTS

The Carnival in Galaxidi is known for its "Flour War," where people throw colored flour at each other.

Many wear old white clothes that get covered in all the colors, making everything look like a big rainbow!

The Carnival in Zakynthos is very special because of the "omilies." These are like little plays or funny shows performed right on the street!

Actors and musicians dress up in costumes, tell silly stories, sing songs, and make everyone laugh.

In Greece, we celebrate Agios Vasilis on New Year's Day, while Christmas is for celebrating Jesus. Agios Vasilis is like Santa Claus. He is a kind old man with a white beard who brings gifts to children.

Kourabiedes are tasty cookies that are covered with powdered sugar, making them look like little snowballs.

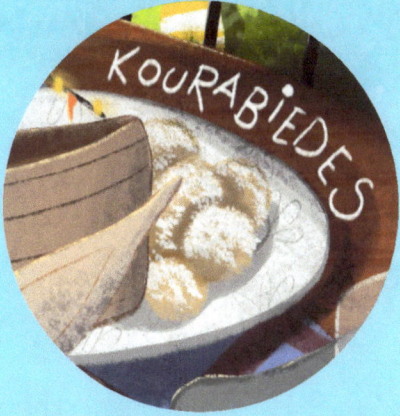

Melomakarona are sweet treats covered in honey and sprinkled with walnuts.

Think you know the story?

TAKE THE
QUIZ

1. What is a name day?
a) A day to play outside
b) A special day for someone named after a saint
c) A day to eat cake

2. What do people say to keep bad luck away in Greece?
a) "Go away! Go away! Go away!"
b) "ftou, ftou, ftou!"
c) "Good luck, good luck, good luck!"

3. What is celebrated on the 28th of October in Greece?
a) A national holiday when Greece said "No" to the Italian invaders during World War II
b) A party for Agios Vasilis
c) A celebration of spring

4. What is hidden inside the Vasilopita cake?
a) A coin
b) A toy
c) A card

Answers
1.B 2.B 3.A 4.A

Reviews are valuable to other readers as well as to authors.
If you enjoyed the book, would you kindly consider reviewing it?
Thank you for your support!

Tag Kassi on Social Media.
She would love to hear from you!

🌐 www.adventuresomewords.com

✉ drkassi@adventuresomewords.com

📷 @stories.by.kassi

f @authorkassipsifogeorgou

Our Very Greek Traditions and A Few Superstitions

About the Author

Kassi is an award-winning author and neuroscientist. As a mother to three lively boys, she finds daily inspiration in the whirlwind of questions, laughter, and bedtime books with her kids, moments she would never trade for the world.

Curiosity and adventure began early in Kassi's own childhood, and that spirit runs through all her stories. Drawing on her background in brain science, Kassi crafts picture books that help young readers grow confident, kind, and uniquely themselves. Whether it's snuggling up to read before bed or exploring new cultures, her characters leap off the page, facing big feelings and celebrating simple joys.

Her "Grow as You Go" series is loved by families and teachers for its playful approach to emotional and social skills, while her "My Greek Roots" stories welcome readers into the lively rhythms of Greek tradition and storytelling.

Living in England with her husband and three children, Kassi loves sharing stories in schools and community spaces. Each book is designed to be a small adventure, inviting children and families everywhere to discover what makes them strong, smart, and ready for life's journey.

About the Illustrator

I'm Laura Mocelin, illustrator and architect living in the north of Rio Grande do Sul, Brasil. I was born in 1996 in Santa Catarina and since then I introduced art in my life in many different ways.

My graduation in architecture and urbanism helped a lot to develop myself as an artist, especially regarding to space, time and dimensions. I always liked to draw on paper, with paint and brushes. But digital art won my heart due to the immense amount of possibilities it gives artists, besides allowing for a more in depth study of light, color and stroke. Today I illustrate mainly children's books, which take me back to my childhood and make me see life in a different way.

You Might Also Like

Our Very Greek Easter: A very Orthodox Easter

STORY MONSTERS APPROVED

*** Tom's family is flying to Greece for Easter to visit Yiayia, Papou and the rest of their extended family. He's so excited to get acquainted with all the Greek traditions of the Holy Week. So, he writes a letter to his best friend describing what he and his brothers did every day, starting from Lazarus Saturday to Easter Sunday.***

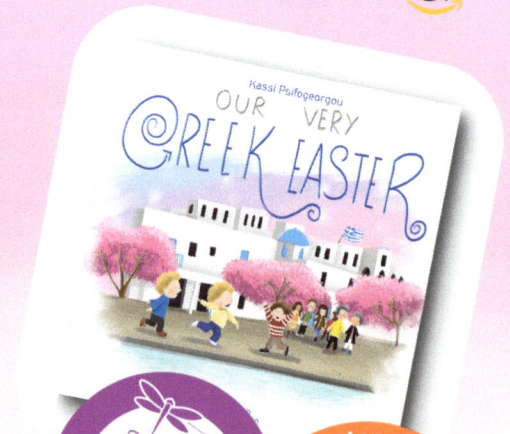

Travel to Greece through this gorgeously illustrated book and learn about the Holy Week in Greek Culture from a Christian perspective. Read about the wonderful traditions that still carry on and the delicious Greek meals planned for the special days!

This book is a keepsake gift that children can enjoy all over the world, focused on the Greek Orthodox Easter.

You Might Also Like

Our Very Greek Summer: And a very Greek Baptism

Alina and her mom have been invited to a baptism in Greece over the summer by their close friends, the Papadopoulos family.

Get ready for an enchanting journey through this stunningly illustrated story, and read about world-famous Greek hospitality! Learn about a traditional Greek baptism, from the godparents' important role to the celebratory feast and dancing called "gledi".

This book is a keepsake gift that children can enjoy all over the world, focused on the Greek 'philoxenia' and the Greek Orthodox Baptism.

On Amazon

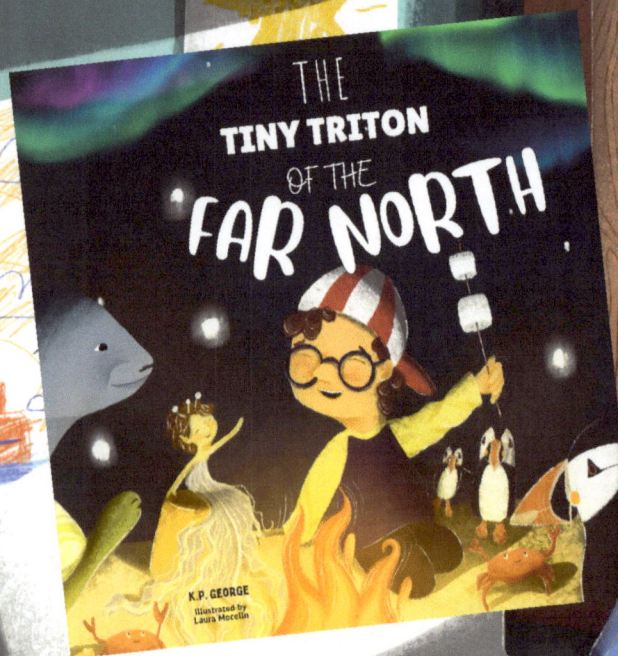

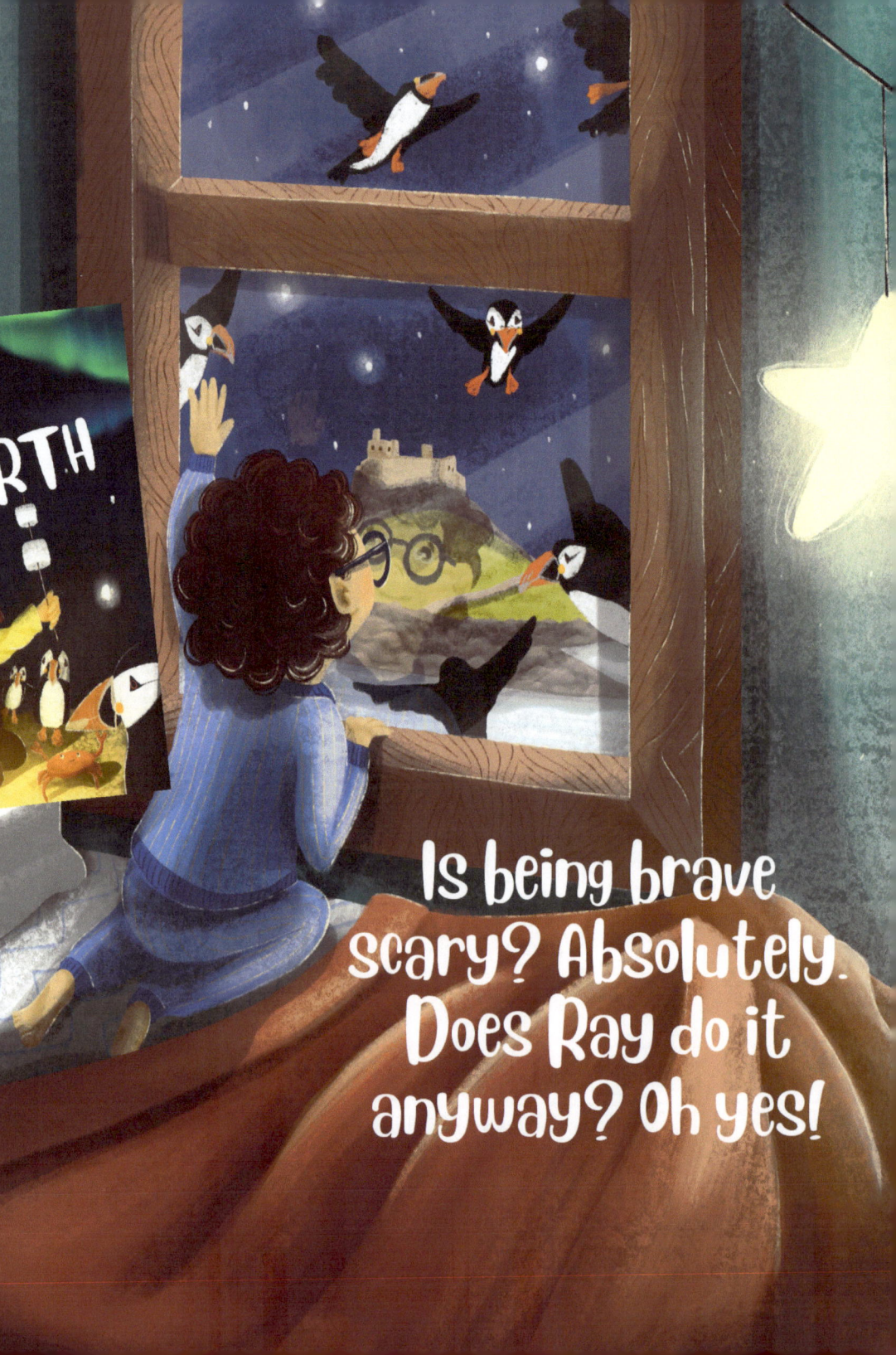

Is being brave scary? Absolutely.
Does Ray do it anyway? Oh yes!

Landmarks On The Move

*** All around the world, landmarks are disappearing. Can the kids figure out where the landmarks have gone and what they're trying to say before history is forgotten for good?

A funny, globe-trotting mystery that turns geography into an unforgettable adventure.***

WITH GEOGRAPHY FACTS

On Amazon **a**

Story Monsters® Approved!
WINNER

Available in English and as a bilingual English-Spanish edition!

MEET THE SKY SIBLINGS

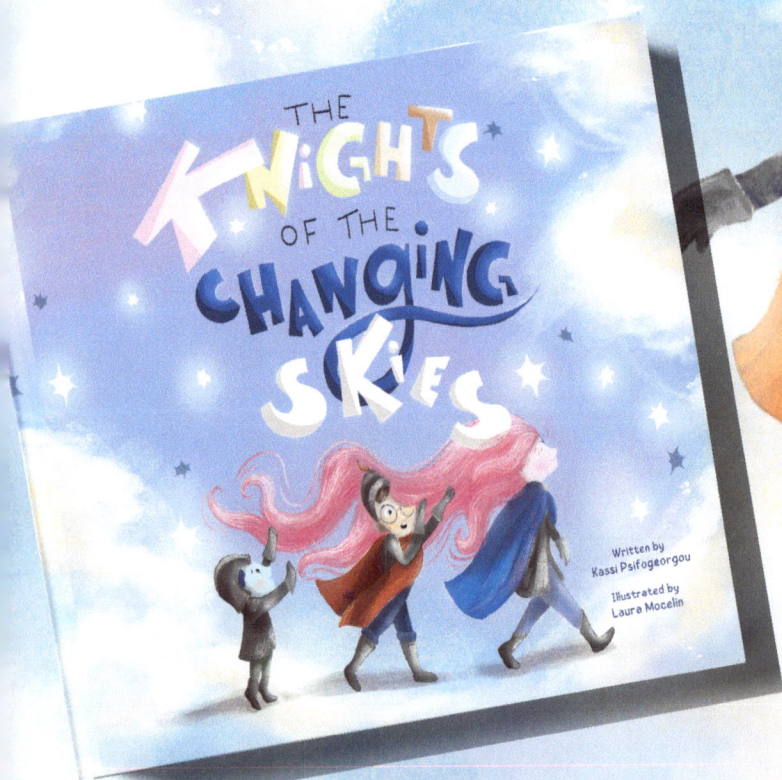

THE **KNiGHTS** OF THE **CHANGING SKiES**

Written by
Kassi Psifogeorgou

Illustrated by
Laura Mocelin

"Rain, Cloud, and Wind aren't ordinary children; they're the Knights of the Changing Skies. When they argue, snow falls, storms rage, and autumn winds roar. But when they laugh and get along, spring blossoms and summer shines brighter than ever."

A story about
growth mindset

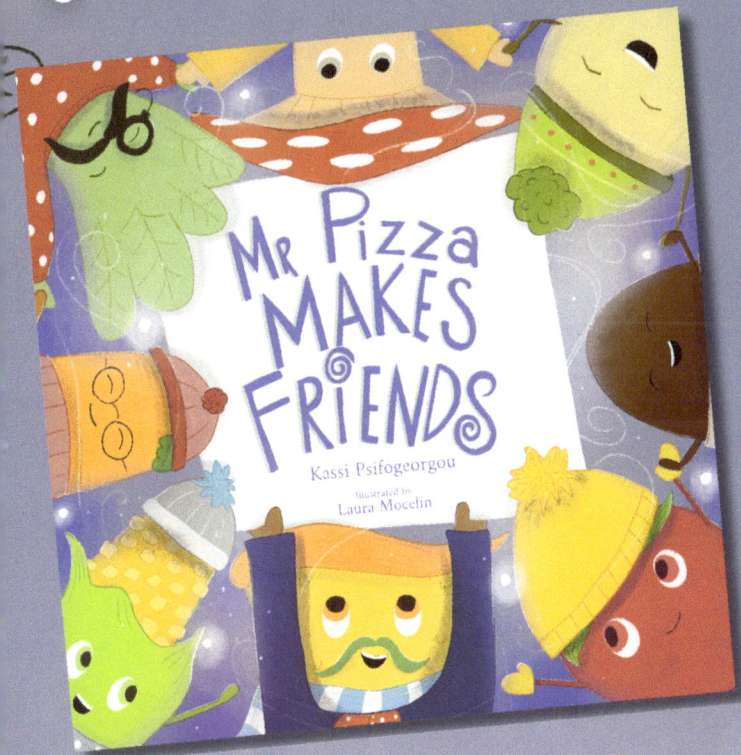

**Mr Pizza
MAKES
FRIENDS**

Kassi Psifogeorgou

Illustrated by
Laura Mocelin

Mr Pizza is a plain slice–just cheese and crust. Nothing fancy at all. At first, Mr Pizza feels a bit lost in a world of flashy toppings.

But when others invite him to play, something surprising happens–olives become buttons, mushrooms form a bow tie, and spinach turns into a moustache. Bit by bit, Mr Pizza discovers he truly belongs.

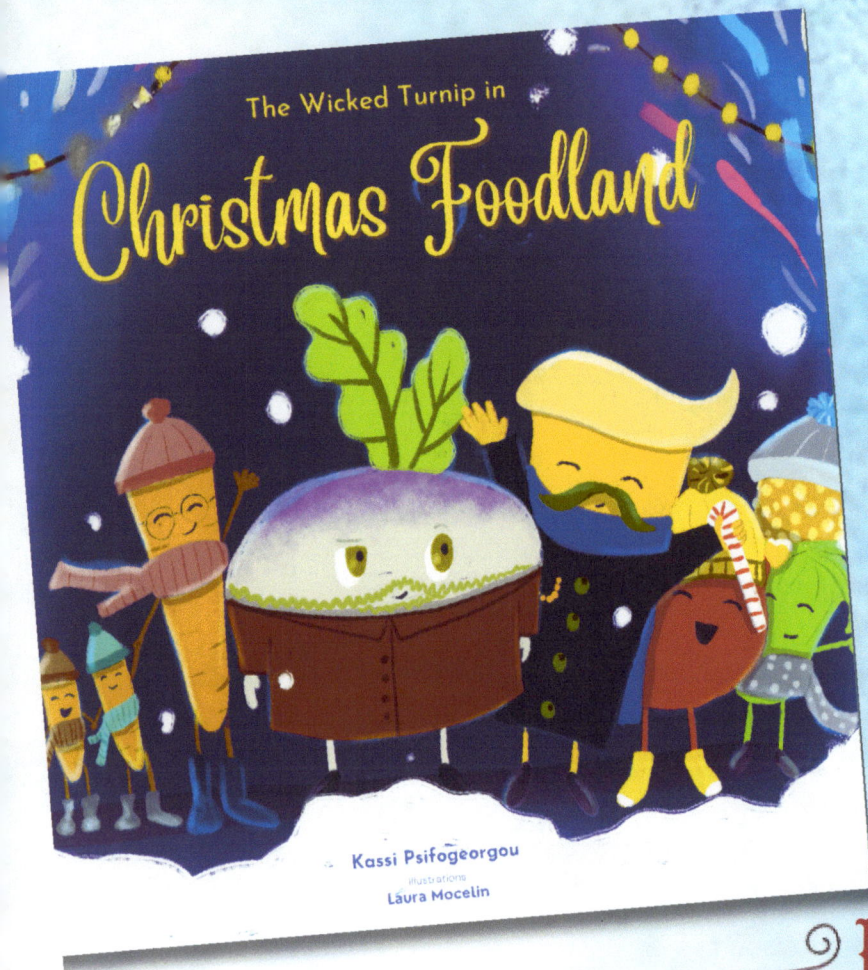

The Wicked Turnip in

Christmas Foodland

Kassi Psifogeorgou

Illustrations
Laura Mocelin

FOLLOW THE

MISCHIEF
IN FOODLAND

CAN ONE GRUMPY VEG
HELP CHRISTMAS
AFTER ALL?